Love, GRIT & Grace

Growth Journal

Copyright © 2022 by Amanda Martin

Published by Kudu Publishing

All rights reserved. No portion of this book may be reproduced, stored in a retrieval system, or transmitted in any form or by any means—electronic, mechanical, photocopy, recording, scanning, or other—except for brief quotations in critical reviews or articles, without prior written permission of the author.

For foreign and subsidiary rights, contact the author.

Cover design by: Sara Young

Author photo on cover: Maggie LaFave

ISBN: 978-1-959095-11-8   1 2 3 4 5 6 7 8 9 10

Printed in the United States of America

A LOVE NOTE WRITTEN BY

AMANDA ELIZABETH MARTIN

Love, GRIT & Grace

Growth Journal

A story on growing through
life's messy grief

KUDU

CONTENTS

Introduction: The Road That Led Me To You 6

Darkest Days 10

Grief 18

Children & Parenting 24

Getting Through the Feelings 30

New Perspective 36

On You 40

Growth & Change 46

Forgiveness 52

The Future Is Bright 58

A LOVE NOTE WRITTEN BY
AMANDA ELIZABETH MARTIN

Love, GRIT & Grace

A true story about growing through life's messy grief

Introduction: The Road That Led Me To You

―♥―

"Some days I still don't know how we ever made it to where we are."
—Amanda Martin

READING TIME

As you read "Introduction: The Road That Led Me To You" in Love, Grit & Grace, reflect on the questions and scriptures.

REFLECT AND TAKE ACTION:

Take time to think about the road that has led you to where you are now. . . .

_____
_____
_____
_____
_____
_____

What are some parts of your story or paths you've taken for which you're grateful? Be specific.

_____
_____
_____
_____
_____
_____

What are some parts of your story or paths you've taken that you wish you could re-do or avoid altogether? What makes you feel this way?

_____
_____
_____
_____
_____
_____

Love, Grit & Grace: **GROWTH JOURNAL**

> *And we know that in all things God works for the good of those who love him, who have been called according to his purpose.*
> *—Romans 8:28*

Consider the scripture above and answer the following questions:

Do you think God can use even the worst of situations for good? Have you ever seen this happen?

_____
_____
_____
_____

What do you think it means when the verse talks about those 'who have been called according to [God's] purpose'? Have you been called according to God's purpose?

_____
_____
_____
_____

Do you think there's any scenario in which God doesn't create good out of bad situations? Does He ever let pain persist without reason?

_____
_____
_____

How can you see God's hand along your path? Have you seen or felt Him move in the situations you disliked as well?

_____
_____
_____
_____

How would your life look different if you hadn't gone through what you went through? Do you think you would be as strong as you are now without those trials?

_____
_____
_____
_____

Do you think your plan for your life is better than God's plan? Do you ever doubt His plan for your life?

_____
_____
_____
_____

Do you ever struggle to see the purpose in the pain that you experience? Have you ever doubted or become angry with the Lord for this pain?

_____
_____
_____
_____

Darkest Days

"You can take your darkest days and
use them as your stepping stones to
a brighter and better future."
—Amanda Martin

READING TIME

As you read "Darkest Days" in Love, Grit & Grace, reflect on the questions and scriptures.

REFLECT AND TAKE ACTION:

What have been some of the darkest days of your life?

_____
_____
_____
_____
_____
_____

When you think about the days and situations you listed above, how do you feel? Sad? Angry? Regretful? Guilty? List all the emotions that apply.

_____
_____
_____
_____
_____
_____

Do you think these dark days will serve a purpose for your life down the road? Why or why not?

_____
_____
_____
_____
_____
_____

*But now, this is what
the LORD says —*

he who created you, Jacob,

he who formed you, Israel:

"Do not fear, for I have redeemed you;

*I have summoned you
by name; you are mine.*

When you pass through the waters,

I will be with you;

and when you pass through the rivers,

they will not sweep over you.

When you walk through the fire,

you will not be burned;

*the flames will not set
you ablaze. . . ."*

—Isaiah 43:1-2

Consider the scripture above and answer the following questions:

What are these verses talking about when they speak of passing through waters and rivers and walking through the fire? Have you ever done anything like this?

_____
_____
_____
_____
_____
_____
_____
_____
_____
_____

According to this verse, how will we not be burned by fire and swept away by water? Is there any other way to survive these events?

_____
_____
_____
_____
_____
_____
_____
_____
_____
_____

*The LORD is my shepherd,
I lack nothing.*

*He makes me lie down
in green pastures,*

he leads me beside quiet waters,

he refreshes my soul.

He guides me along the right paths

for his name's sake.

Even though I walk

through the darkest valley,

I will fear no evil,

for you are with me;

your rod and your staff,

they comfort me.

—Psalm 23:1-4

Consider the scripture above and answer the following questions:

What is the significance of the phrase, 'Even though I walk through the darkest valley'?

_____
_____
_____
_____
_____

Why do you think David called God his shepherd in this passage?

_____
_____
_____
_____
_____
_____

This verse states that God guides us along the right paths. Have you ever felt like God was taking you down the wrong path before you reached the end of it?

_____
_____
_____
_____
_____
_____

Can you see God's grace and beauty in any of the hard parts of your journey?

___

Have you ever seen someone else lean on God amidst the darkest days of their life? If so, who was it, and how did they respond to the adversity they were experiencing?

___

Do you think you've healed from the darkest days of your life? If so, what helped you heal? If not, what's holding you back?

___

Grief

"Grief can change you for the better if you allow it. It can help you see the world and your life in a whole new light. It can help you grow and evolve."
—Amanda Martin

READING TIME

As you read "Grief" in *Love, Grit & Grace*, reflect on the questions and scriptures.

REFLECT AND TAKE ACTION:

What or who have you grieved? A loved one? A broken marriage? A crushed dream? List everything that applies.

_____
_____
_____
_____
_____
_____

How does it feel to know that God remembers and understands each of your sorrows?

_____
_____
_____
_____
_____

What are some emotions you've experienced while grieving that were uncomfortable?

_____
_____
_____
_____
_____

> *The LORD is close to the brokenhearted*
> *and saves those who are crushed in spirit.*
> *—Psalm 34:18*

Consider the scripture above and answer the following questions:

Have you ever been brokenhearted? Did you feel like the Lord was close to you in those moments?

_____
_____
_____
_____
_____

In your own words, what does it mean to be crushed in spirit?

_____
_____
_____
_____

Why do you think God is close to the brokenhearted and saves those who are crushed in spirit? What does this reveal about His character?

_____
_____
_____
_____
_____

If you say, "The LORD is my refuge," and you make the Most High your dwelling, no harm will overtake you, no disaster will come near your tent. For he will command his angels concerning you to guard you in all your ways; they will lift you up in their hands, so that you will not strike your foot against a stone. You will tread on the lion and the cobra; you will trample the great lion and the serpent.
—Psalm 91:9-13

Consider the scripture above and answer the following questions:

What does it mean to take refuge in the Most High?

_____
_____
_____

Have you ever seen proof of this verse in your life or in someone else's life? Describe the experience.

_____
_____
_____

What were some expectations you had about the grieving process that you discovered weren't true for you?

_____
_____
_____

Love, Grit & Grace: GROWTH JOURNAL | 21

How has your grief changed you? Do you think the change is a positive or negative?

___

Since grieving, how has your personal view of grief shifted?

___

Are there any aspects of grief that surprised you? What were they?

___

Children & Parenting

"I did what I thought was best and
learned as each day went on."
—Amanda Martin

READING TIME

As you read "Children & Parenting" in *Love, Grit & Grace*, reflect on the questions and scriptures.

REFLECT AND TAKE ACTION:

What aspects of parenting have you found to be the most challenging while battling grief?

_____
_____
_____
_____
_____
_____

How have your children handled grief? Depending on their ages, do you feel that you're equipping them with the tools they need to battle grief alongside you?

_____
_____
_____
_____
_____
_____

What areas of your parenting do you think suffer the most while you are in the grieving process? How can you strengthen these areas?

_____
_____
_____
_____
_____
_____

> *He tends his flocks like a shepherd: He gathers the lambs in his arms And carries them close to his heart; He gently leads those that have young.*
> *—Isaiah 40:11*

Consider the scripture above and answer the following questions:

Take time to read this verse and let it settle into your heart. God isn't asking you to figure out all the details of your journey on your own. He wants you to lean on Him as He gently leads you and your children.

_____
_____
_____

How do you feel knowing God wants to 'gently lead' you and your children?

_____
_____
_____

What do you think 'gently lead' means?

_____
_____
_____

Do you think parents should strive to be gentle leaders in certain situations? Why or why not?

_____
_____
_____

> *The Spirit of the Sovereign LORD is on me, because the LORD has anointed me to proclaim good news to the poor. He has sent me to bind up the brokenhearted, to proclaim freedom for the captives and release from darkness for the prisoners...*
> —Isaiah 61:1

Consider the scripture above and answer the following questions:

What do you think is the meaning of the above verse?

_____
_____
_____
_____

Earlier, we read that God is close to the brokenhearted. Do you think this verse reveals His mercy for those who have been hurt?

_____
_____
_____
_____

What does it mean and look like to have the Spirit of the Sovereign LORD on you?

_____
_____
_____
_____

What are some ways you can connect with your kids?

_____
_____
_____
_____

How can you help your children through the 'darkest days' of their lives?

_____
_____
_____
_____

Make a practical, seven-day plan outlining the time you will spend with your children and the things you will talk to them about and empower them with:

1. _____
_____
_____
_____

2. _____
_____
_____
_____

3. _____
_____
_____
_____

4. _____
_____
_____
_____

5. _____
_____
_____
_____

6. _____
_____
_____
_____

7. _____
_____
_____
_____
_____

Getting Through the Feelings

"The momentary discomfort will fade away after you begin to discover the comfort of healing."
—Amanda Martin

READING TIME

As you read "Getting Through the Feelings" in *Love, Grit & Grace*, reflect on the questions and scriptures.

REFLECT AND TAKE ACTION:

What are some big emotions and feelings you've faced in the past?

_____
_____
_____
_____
_____
_____

What are some of your favorite scriptures and quotes that you can go to when you're face-to-face with overwhelming feelings? Come up with one to three.

_____
_____
_____
_____
_____
_____

What are some practical steps you can take to navigate through the unexpected, uncomfortable feelings that may arise in an adverse situations?

_____
_____
_____
_____
_____
_____

Love, Grit & Grace: GROWTH JOURNAL | 31

*So do not fear, for I am with you;
do not be dismayed, for I am your God.
I will strengthen you and help you;
I will uphold you with my
righteous right hand.
—Isaiah 41:10*

Consider the scripture above and answer the following questions:

Do you ever forget that God is with you due to overwhelming feelings of fear, guilt, or uncertainty?

_____
_____
_____
_____
_____
_____

Has God ever strengthened and helped you in a situation when you called upon Him? Describe the situation.

_____
_____
_____
_____
_____
_____

> *Unless the LORD had given me help, I would soon have dwelt in the silence of death. When I said, "My foot is slipping," your unfailing love, LORD, supported me, your consolation brought me joy.*
> —Psalm 94:17-19

Consider the scripture above and answer the following questions:

What are different ways—in your life and the lives of others—you've seen the Lord intervene and provide help?

_____
_____
_____
_____
_____
_____
_____
_____

Do you think God is faithful when we go to Him in honesty and weakness?

_____
_____
_____
_____
_____
_____
_____

What does 'unfailing love' mean? What does it look like in action?

_____
_____
_____
_____
_____
_____

What does it mean to 'be still'? What does 'being still' look like for you specifically?

_____
_____
_____
_____
_____
_____
_____
_____

In your own words, what does it mean to just 'be'? Where do you go to just be?

_____
_____
_____
_____
_____
_____
_____

Have you ever been able to connect big, uncontrollable emotions that arise in a situation to another event or issue?

_____
_____
_____
_____
_____
_____
_____

At what point do you think these big emotions become a problem?

_____
_____
_____
_____
_____
_____
_____

New Perspective

"I had to let go of the vision I had for our life together as a family. It would now look totally different than what I had ever dreamed it would look like."
—Amanda Martin

READING TIME

As you read "New Perspective" in *Love, Grit & Grace,* reflect on the questions and scriptures.

REFLECT AND TAKE ACTION:

How can God use your pain and disappointments for a greater purpose?

_____
_____
_____
_____
_____
_____

Since going through loss, disappointment, and pain, do you look at your life differently? If yes, how so?

_____
_____
_____
_____
_____
_____
_____

Do you think your pain has helped you grow mentally and spiritually? Why or why not?

_____
_____
_____
_____
_____
_____

> *I will give you a new heart and put a new spirit in you; I will remove from you your heart of stone and give you a heart of flesh.*
> —*Ezekiel 36:26*

Consider the scripture above and answer the following questions:

What is the difference between the heart and the spirit? Why do we have to receive both a new heart and a new spirit?

_____
_____
_____
_____
_____

What does a heart of stone look like when compared to a heart of flesh?

_____
_____
_____
_____
_____

Do you ever feel like external events have hardened your heart into a heart of stone? What is the current state of your heart?

_____
_____
_____
_____
_____

> *You will keep in perfect peace those whose minds are steadfast, because they trust in you.*
> *—Isaiah 26:3*

Consider the scripture above and answer the following questions:

What does this verse mean when it talks of 'perfect peace'? Do you live with perfect peace right now?

_____
_____

What do you put your trust in other than God? What or Whom do you trust in the most?

_____
_____

Are there ways you can give hope to others by sharing your story? Who could benefit from hearing about your journey?

_____
_____

Are there parts of your loss, pain, or disappointment for which you can be grateful? If so, what are they?

_____
_____

How has your perspective on loss changed since coming out the other side of the pain you endured?

_____
_____

On You

♡

"Allow yourself time to come together and be rebuilt. Give yourself a moment to catch your breath and realign with your new life."
—Amanda Martin

READING TIME

As you read "On You" in Love, Grit & Grace, *reflect on the questions and scriptures.*

REFLECT AND TAKE ACTION:

What area(s) of your life do you feel have been the most impacted by the loss you experienced?

_____
_____
_____
_____
_____
_____

Do you think this situation could be a new beginning for you? Why or why not?

_____
_____
_____
_____
_____
_____

Can you take a risk today that you would not have been able to take beforehand? If so, what kind of risk is it?

_____
_____
_____
_____
_____
_____

> *May the God of hope fill you with all joy and peace as you trust him, so that you may overflow with hope by the power of the Holy Spirit.*
> *—Romans 15:13*

Consider the scripture above and answer the following questions:

How would you expect someone who's overflowing with hope to live their life? Do you live life this way?

_____
_____
_____
_____
_____
_____
_____
_____
_____

What is the prerequisite to being filled with joy and peace, according to this verse?

_____
_____
_____
_____
_____
_____
_____
_____
_____

Therefore, I urge you, brothers and sisters, in view of God's mercy, to offer your bodies as a living sacrifice, holy and pleasing to God — this is your true and proper worship. Do not conform to the pattern of this world, but be transformed by the renewing of your mind. Then you will be able to test and prove what God's will is — his good, pleasing and perfect will.
—*Romans 12:1-2*

Consider the scripture above and answer the following questions:

What in your life do you need to change in order to make your body a living sacrifice, pleasing to God?

_____
_____
_____
_____
_____
_____

What does it mean to renew your mind? How are we transformed by the renewing of our minds?

_____
_____
_____
_____
_____
_____

Despite your negative feelings, how can you show up for yourself?

___

In what areas of your life do you need to start trusting yourself again?

___

What parts of your story—if any—are you struggling to own? What's stopping you from embracing these parts of your journey?

___

_____

_____

_____

_____

_____

_____

What parts of your story that were out of your control do you need to release?

_____

_____

_____

_____

_____

_____

_____

_____

_____

_____

Growth & Change

"All of the roads you took when you appeared to be lost, are the exact roads that have led you home, to the new you."
—Amanda Martin

READING TIME

As you read "Growth & Change" in *Love, Grit & Grace*, reflect on the questions and scriptures.

REFLECT AND TAKE ACTION:

In what areas of your life have you felt the most change?

_____
_____
_____
_____
_____
_____
_____

Do you think change is necessary? Where would you be if you hadn't changed since experiencing loss?

_____
_____
_____
_____
_____
_____
_____

Can you identify areas of your life that have experienced growth? What are they?

_____
_____
_____
_____
_____
_____

> *Not only so, but we also glory in our sufferings, because we know that suffering produces perseverance; perseverance, character; and character, hope. And hope does not put us to shame, because God's love has been poured out into our hearts through the Holy Spirit, who has been given to us.*
> —Romans 5:3-5

Consider the scripture above and answer the following questions:

How is there glory in suffering? When have you seen evidence of this?

_____
_____
_____
_____
_____
_____

Do you think you can have character and hope without suffering and perseverance? Why or why not?

_____
_____
_____
_____
_____
_____
_____

Not that I have already obtained all this, or have already arrived at my goal, but I press on to take hold of that for which Christ Jesus took hold of me. Brothers and sisters, I do not consider myself yet to have taken hold of it. But one thing I do: Forgetting what is behind and straining toward what is ahead, I press on toward the goal to win the prize for which God has called me heavenward in Christ Jesus.
—Philippians 3:12-14

Consider the scripture above and answer the following questions:

Do you consider yourself to have taken ahold of the purpose God has put you on a path to reach? Why or why not?

_____
_____
_____
_____
_____

Do you let your past affect your pursuit of purpose? If so, how?

_____
_____
_____
_____
_____
_____

What is the prize that Paul speaks of towards the end of this passage?

_____
_____
_____
_____
_____
_____
_____

In what additional areas of your life would you like to experience growth?

_____
_____
_____
_____
_____
_____
_____

What are practical steps you can start taking today to ensure growth in these areas?

_____
_____
_____
_____

_____
_____
_____
_____
_____

What areas of your life would you like to change? How would you like to change them?

_____
_____
_____
_____
_____
_____
_____

What are some practical ways you can implement the changes you discussed above?

_____
_____
_____
_____
_____
_____
_____

Forgiveness

♡

"Dumping the guilt begins with acknowledging how you feel. Give yourself permission and space to feel the relief."
—Amanda Martin

READING TIME

As you read "Forgiveness" in Love, Grit & Grace, reflect on the questions and scriptures.

REFLECT AND TAKE ACTION:

Which parts of your story have you struggled to forgive yourself or others?

_____
_____
_____
_____
_____
_____

Can you forgive someone else without receiving an apology from them? Why or why not?

_____
_____
_____
_____
_____
_____

What is your personal definition of forgiveness? What does forgiveness mean to you?

_____
_____
_____
_____
_____
_____

> *Bear with each other and forgive one another if any of you has a grievance against someone. Forgive as the Lord forgave you.*
> *—Colossians 3:13*

Consider the scripture above and answer the following questions:

Do you ever struggle to obey this verse? When have you been hesitant to forgive someone else—or yourself?

_____
_____
_____
_____
_____
_____
_____
_____

Why should we be so quick to forgive as Christians?

_____
_____
_____
_____
_____
_____
_____
_____

> *Trust in the LORD with all your heart*
> *and lean not on your own understanding;*
> *in all your ways submit to him, and*
> *he will make your paths straight.*
> *—Proverbs 3:5-6*

Consider the scripture above and answer the following questions:

What does it mean to trust in the Lord with ALL your heart? How would someone's life look if they lived like this?

_____
_____
_____
_____
_____
_____
_____
_____

What areas of your life do you still need to submit to God, if any? Your career? Your marriage? Your parenting?

_____
_____
_____
_____
_____
_____
_____

Do you think God will make our paths straight if we refuse to submit to Him? Why or why not?

_____
_____
_____
_____
_____
_____
_____

What role does guilt play in your journey of self-forgiveness? What do you feel guilty about right now?

_____
_____
_____
_____
_____
_____
_____

Is there any circumstance in which you shouldn't forgive someone who has wronged you?

_____
_____
_____
_____
_____
_____
_____

Do you think forgiveness is an integral part of the healing process? Why or why not?

_____
_____
_____
_____
_____
_____
_____

How do you think you will feel when you finally choose to forgive yourself and others fully? What's holding you back?

_____
_____
_____
_____
_____
_____
_____

The Future Is Bright

"*Give yourself permission to dream again.*"
—Amanda Martin

READING TIME

As you read "The Future Is Bright" in *Love, Grit & Grace*, reflect on the questions and scriptures.

REFLECT AND TAKE ACTION:

What do you want your future to look like? Do you think God wants the same for you?

_____
_____
_____
_____
_____
_____

Do you believe God has goodness in store for you? Back up your answer with scripture.

_____
_____
_____
_____
_____
_____
_____
_____

Can you see God working in your life to grant you a brighter future? In what ways is He working?

_____
_____
_____
_____
_____
_____

> *"For I know the plans I have for you,"*
> *declares the LORD, "plans to prosper*
> *you and not to harm you, plans to*
> *give you a hope and a future."*
> *—Jeremiah 29:11*

Consider the scripture above and answer the following questions:

Do you ever doubt the reality and goodness of God's plans for your life? Why or why not?

_____
_____
_____
_____

Are you willing to cast aside your plans and embrace the bigger, better plans God has for you?

_____
_____
_____
_____

How do you define prosperity? Are there different ways to prosper besides just financially?

_____
_____
_____
_____

> *Therefore we do not lose heart. Though outwardly we are wasting away, yet inwardly we are being renewed day by day. For our light and momentary troubles are achieving for us an eternal glory that far outweighs them all. So we fix our eyes not on what is seen, but on what is unseen, since what is seen is temporary, but what is unseen is eternal.*
> —2 Corinthians 4:16-18

Consider the scripture above and answer the following questions:

What is the 'eternal glory' Paul writes about in these verses? Why is it so much more important than our momentary troubles?

_____
_____
_____
_____
_____
_____
_____

What are the 'seen' and the 'unseen' Paul writes to the Corinthians about in this passage?

_____
_____
_____
_____
_____

Take time to think back over your life and remember all the times God has shown up and come through for you. List some of the times you've seen Him intervene in your life:

_____
_____
_____
_____
_____
_____
_____
_____
_____
_____
_____
_____
_____
_____
_____

Do you believe in God to keep the promises He has made to you? Are you living your life accordingly?

_____
_____
_____
_____
_____

Create a dream board. Attach pictures, quotes, scriptures, and drawings to a poster or board that will remind you daily about the brighter future God has in store for you.

www.ingramcontent.com/pod-product-compliance
Lightning Source LLC
Chambersburg PA
CBHW062123080426
42734CB00012B/2961